THIS FUCKING JOURNAL BELONGS TO

_____

Date:_____

Things That Pissed Me Off Today

_____

_____

_____

_____

_____

Things That Made Me Laugh Today

_____

_____

_____

_____

_____

My Mood Today

Scale of 1-8 (8 being, In A Very Bad Mood)

Today's Fucking Tasks

I'm So Glad I Didn't...

I'm So Relieved I Did..

SHIT I NEED TO DO TODAY

1
2
3
4
5

Date:_____

Things That Stressed Me Out Today

_____

_____

_____

_____

_____

_____

Things That Calmed Me Down Today

_____

_____

_____

_____

_____

My Mood Today

Scale of 1-8 (8 being, In A Very Bad Mood)

Today's Fucking Thoughts

People That Stressed Me Out Today

Draw Something Here

Date:_____

Things That Pissed Me Off Today

_____
_____
_____
_____
_____
_____

Things That Made Me Smile Today

_____
_____
_____
_____
_____
_____

My Mood Today

Scale of 1-8 (8 being, In A Very Bad Mood)

Today's Fucking Tasks

I'm So Glad I Didn't...

I'm So Relieved I Did..

SHIT I NEED TO DO TODAY

1
2
3
4
5

Date:_____

Things That Angered Me Today

_____

_____

_____

_____

_____

_____

Things That Calmed Me Down Today

_____

_____

_____

_____

_____

_____

My Mood Today

Scale of 1-8 (8 being, In A Very Bad Mood)

Today's Fucking Thoughts

People I Want To Strangle Today

Draw Something Here

Date:_____

Things That Pissed Me Off Today

_____

_____

_____

_____

_____

_____

Things That Made Me Smile Today

_____

_____

_____

_____

_____

My Mood Today

Scale of 1-8 (8 being, In A Very Bad Mood)

Today's Fucking Tasks

I'm So Glad I Didn't...

I'm So Relieved I Did..

SHIT I NEED TO DO TODAY

1
2
3
4
5

Date:_____

Things That Pissed Me Off Today

_____

_____

_____

_____

_____

_____

Things That Made Me Smile Today

_____

_____

_____

_____

_____

My Mood Today

Scale of 1-8 (8 being, In A Very Bad Mood)

Today's Fucking Thoughts

People I Want To Strangle Today

Draw Something Here

Date:_____

Things That Pissed Me Off Today

_____

_____

_____

_____

_____

_____

Things That Made Me Smile Today

_____

_____

_____

_____

_____

My Mood Today

Scale of 1-8 (8 being, In A Very Bad Mood)

Today's Fucking Tasks

I'm So Glad I Didn't...

I'm So Relieved I Did..

SHIT I NEED TO DO TODAY

1
2
3
4
5

Date:_____

Things That Pissed Me Off Today

_____
_____
_____
_____
_____
_____

Things That Made Me Smile Today

_____
_____
_____
_____
_____

My Mood Today

Scale of 1-8 (8 being, In A Very Bad Mood)

Today's Fucking Thoughts

People I Want To Strangle Today

Draw Something Here

Date:_____

Things That Pissed Me Off Today

_____

_____

_____

_____

_____

_____

Things That Made Me Smile Today

_____

_____

_____

_____

_____

_____

My Mood Today

Scale of 1-8 (8 being, In A Very Bad Mood)

Today's Fucking Tasks

I'm So Glad I Didn't...

I'm So Relieved I Did..

SHIT I NEED TO DO TODAY

1
2
3
4
5

Date:_____

Things That Pissed Me Off Today

_____

_____

_____

_____

_____

_____

Things That Made Me Smile Today

_____

_____

_____

_____

_____

_____

My Mood Today

Scale of 1-8 (8 being, In A Very Bad Mood)

Today's Fucking Thoughts

◆ ——— • ● ◆ ● • ——— ◆

People I Want To Strangle Today

Draw Something Here

Date:_____

Things That Pissed Me Off Today

_____
_____
_____
_____
_____
_____

Things That Made Me Smile Today

_____
_____
_____
_____
_____
_____

My Mood Today

Scale of 1-8 (8 being, In A Very Bad Mood)

Today's Fucking Tasks

I'm So Glad I Didn't...

I'm So Relieved I Did..

SHIT I NEED TO DO TODAY

1
2
3
4
5

Date:_____

Things That Pissed Me Off Today

_____

_____

_____

_____

_____

_____

Things That Made Me Smile Today

_____

_____

_____

_____

_____

My Mood Today

Scale of 1-8 (8 being, In A Very Bad Mood)

Today's Fucking Thoughts

People I Want To Strangle Today

Draw Something Here

Date:_____

Things That Pissed Me Off Today

_____

_____

_____

_____

_____

_____

Things That Made Me Smile Today

_____

_____

_____

_____

_____

_____

My Mood Today

Scale of 1-8 (8 being, In A Very Bad Mood)

Today's Fucking Tasks

I'm So Glad I Didn't...

I'm So Relieved I Did..

SHIT I NEED TO DO TODAY

1
2
3
4
5

Date:_____

Things That Pissed Me Off Today

_____
_____
_____
_____
_____
_____

Things That Made Me Smile Today

_____
_____
_____
_____
_____
_____

My Mood Today

Scale of 1-8 (8 being, In A Very Bad Mood)

Today's Fucking Thoughts

People I Want To Strangle Today

Draw Something Here

Date:_____

Things That Pissed Me Off Today

_____

_____

_____

_____

_____

Things That Made Me Smile Today

_____

_____

_____

_____

_____

My Mood Today

🖕 🖕 🖕 🖕 🖕 🖕 🖕 🖕

Scale of 1-8 (8 being, In A Very Bad Mood)

Today's Fucking Tasks

I'm So Glad I Didn't...

I'm So Relieved I Did..

SHIT I NEED TO DO TODAY

1
2
3
4
5

Date:_____

Things That Pissed Me Off Today

_____

_____

_____

_____

_____

_____

Things That Made Me Smile Today

_____

_____

_____

_____

_____

_____

My Mood Today

Scale of 1-8 (8 being, In A Very Bad Mood)

Today's Fucking Thoughts

People I Want To Strangle Today

Draw Something Here

Date:_____

Things That Pissed Me Off Today

_____

_____

_____

_____

_____

_____

Things That Made Me Smile Today

_____

_____

_____

_____

_____

_____

My Mood Today

Scale of 1-8 (8 being, In A Very Bad Mood)

Today's Fucking Tasks

I'm So Glad I Didn't...

I'm So Relieved I Did..

SHIT I NEED TO DO TODAY

1
2
3
4
5

Date:_____

Things That Pissed Me Off Today

_____

_____

_____

_____

_____

_____

Things That Made Me Smile Today

_____

_____

_____

_____

_____

_____

My Mood Today

Scale of 1-8 (8 being, In A Very Bad Mood)

Today's Fucking Thoughts

People I Want To Strangle Today

Draw Something Here

Date:_____

Things That Pissed Me Off Today

_____

_____

_____

_____

_____

_____

Things That Made Me Smile Today

_____

_____

_____

_____

_____

_____

My Mood Today

👆 👆 👆 👆 👆 👆 👆 👆

Scale of 1-8 (8 being, In A Very Bad Mood)

Today's Fucking Tasks

I'm So Glad I Didn't...

I'm So Relieved I Did..

SHIT I NEED TO DO TODAY

1
2
3
4
5

Date:_____

Things That Pissed Me Off Today

_____
_____
_____
_____
_____
_____

Things That Made Me Smile Today

_____
_____
_____
_____
_____
_____

My Mood Today

Scale of 1-8 (8 being, In A Very Bad Mood)

Today's Fucking Thoughts

People I Want To Strangle Today

Draw Something Here

Date:_____

Things That Pissed Me Off Today

_____

_____

_____

_____

_____

_____

Things That Made Me Smile Today

_____

_____

_____

_____

_____

_____

My Mood Today

Scale of 1-8 (8 being, In A Very Bad Mood)

Today's Fucking Tasks

I'm So Glad I Didn't...

I'm So Relieved I Did..

SHIT I NEED TO DO TODAY

1
2
3
4
5

Date:_____

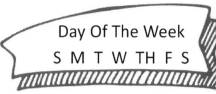

Things That Pissed Me Off Today

_____

_____

_____

_____

_____

_____

Things That Made Me Smile Today

_____

_____

_____

_____

_____

My Mood Today

Scale of 1-8 (8 being, In A Very Bad Mood)

Today's Fucking Thoughts

People I Want To Strangle Today

Draw Something Here

Date:_____

Things That Pissed Me Off Today

_____
_____
_____
_____
_____
_____

Things That Made Me Smile Today

_____
_____
_____
_____
_____
_____

My Mood Today

Scale of 1-8 (8 being, In A Very Bad Mood)

Today's Fucking Tasks

I'm So Glad I Didn't...

I'm So Relieved I Did..

SHIT I NEED TO DO TODAY

1
2
3
4
5

Date:_____

Things That Pissed Me Off Today

_____

_____

_____

_____

_____

_____

Things That Made Me Smile Today

_____

_____

_____

_____

_____

My Mood Today

Scale of 1-8 (8 being, In A Very Bad Mood)

Today's Fucking Thoughts

People I Want To Strangle Today

Draw Something Here

Date:_____

Things That Pissed Me Off Today

_____

_____

_____

_____

_____

_____

Things That Made Me Smile Today

_____

_____

_____

_____

_____

_____

My Mood Today

Scale of 1-8 (8 being, In A Very Bad Mood)

Today's Fucking Tasks

I'm So Glad I Didn't...

I'm So Relieved I Did..

SHIT I NEED TO DO TODAY

1
2
3
4
5

Date: _____

Things That Pissed Me Off Today

_____

_____

_____

_____

_____

Things That Made Me Smile Today

_____

_____

_____

_____

_____

My Mood Today

Scale of 1-8 (8 being, In A Very Bad Mood)

Today's Fucking Thoughts

People I Want To Strangle Today

Draw Something Here

Date:_____

Things That Pissed Me Off Today

_____

_____

_____

_____

_____

Things That Made Me Smile Today

_____

_____

_____

_____

_____

My Mood Today

Scale of 1-8 (8 being, In A Very Bad Mood)

Today's Fucking Tasks

I'm So Glad I Didn't...

I'm So Relieved I Did..

SHIT I NEED TO DO TODAY

1
2
3
4
5

Date:_____

Things That Pissed Me Off Today

_____
_____
_____
_____
_____
_____

Things That Made Me Smile Today

_____
_____
_____
_____
_____
_____

My Mood Today

Scale of 1-8 (8 being, In A Very Bad Mood)

Today's Fucking Thoughts

People I Want To Strangle Today

Draw Something Here

Date: _____

Things That Pissed Me Off Today

_____

_____

_____

_____

_____

_____

Things That Made Me Smile Today

_____

_____

_____

_____

_____

_____

My Mood Today

Scale of 1-8 (8 being, In A Very Bad Mood)

Today's Fucking Tasks

I'm So Glad I Didn't...

I'm So Relieved I Did..

SHIT I NEED TO DO TODAY

1
2
3
4
5

Date:_____

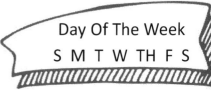
Things That Pissed Me Off Today

_____

_____

_____

_____

_____

_____

Things That Made Me Smile Today

_____

_____

_____

_____

_____

_____

My Mood Today

Scale of 1-8 (8 being, In A Very Bad Mood)

Today's Fucking Thoughts

People I Want To Strangle Today

Draw Something Here

Date:_____

Day Of The Week

S M T W TH F S

Things That Pissed Me Off Today

_____

_____

_____

_____

_____

_____

Things That Made Me Smile Today

_____

_____

_____

_____

_____

_____

My Mood Today

Scale of 1-8 (8 being, In A Very Bad Mood)

Today's Fucking Tasks

I'm So Glad I Didn't...

I'm So Relieved I Did..

SHIT I NEED TO DO TODAY

1
2
3
4
5

Date:_____

Things That Pissed Me Off Today

_____

_____

_____

_____

_____

_____

Things That Made Me Smile Today

_____

_____

_____

_____

_____

_____

My Mood Today

Scale of 1-8 (8 being, In A Very Bad Mood)

Today's Fucking Thoughts

People I Want To Strangle Today

Draw Something Here

Date:_____

Things That Pissed Me Off Today

_____

_____

_____

_____

_____

_____

Things That Made Me Smile Today

_____

_____

_____

_____

_____

My Mood Today

Scale of 1-8 (8 being, In A Very Bad Mood)

Today's Fucking Tasks

I'm So Glad I Didn't...

I'm So Relieved I Did..

SHIT I NEED TO DO TODAY

1
2
3
4
5

Date:_____

Things That Pissed Me Off Today

_____

_____

_____

_____

_____

Things That Made Me Smile Today

_____

_____

_____

_____

_____

My Mood Today

Scale of 1-8 (8 being, In A Very Bad Mood)

Today's Fucking Thoughts

People I Want To Strangle Today

Draw Something Here

Date:_____

Things That Pissed Me Off Today

_____

_____

_____

_____

_____

_____

Things That Made Me Smile Today

_____

_____

_____

_____

_____

_____

My Mood Today

Scale of 1-8 (8 being, In A Very Bad Mood)

Today's Fucking Tasks

I'm So Glad I Didn't...

I'm So Relieved I Did..

SHIT I NEED TO DO TODAY

1
2
3
4
5

Date:_____

Things That Pissed Me Off Today

_____

_____

_____

_____

_____

_____

Things That Made Me Smile Today

_____

_____

_____

_____

_____

_____

My Mood Today

Scale of 1-8 (8 being, In A Very Bad Mood)

Today's Fucking Thoughts

People I Want To Strangle Today

Draw Something Here

Date:_____

Things That Pissed Me Off Today

_____

_____

_____

_____

_____

_____

Things That Made Me Smile Today

_____

_____

_____

_____

_____

_____

My Mood Today

Scale of 1-8 (8 being, In A Very Bad Mood)

Today's Fucking Tasks

I'm So Glad I Didn't...

I'm So Relieved I Did..

SHIT I NEED TO DO TODAY

1
2
3
4
5

Date:_____

Things That Pissed Me Off Today

_____
_____
_____
_____
_____
_____

Things That Made Me Smile Today

_____
_____
_____
_____
_____
_____

My Mood Today

Scale of 1-8 (8 being, In A Very Bad Mood)

Today's Fucking Thoughts

People I Want To Strangle Today

Draw Something Here

Date:_____

Things That Pissed Me Off Today

_____
_____
_____
_____
_____
_____

Things That Made Me Smile Today

_____
_____
_____
_____
_____
_____

My Mood Today

Scale of 1-8 (8 being, In A Very Bad Mood)

Today's Fucking Tasks

I'm So Glad I Didn't...

I'm So Relieved I Did..

SHIT I NEED TO DO TODAY

1
2
3
4
5

Date:_____

Things That Pissed Me Off Today

_____

_____

_____

_____

_____

_____

Things That Made Me Smile Today

_____

_____

_____

_____

_____

_____

My Mood Today

Scale of 1-8 (8 being, In A Very Bad Mood)

Today's Fucking Thoughts

People I Want To Strangle Today

Draw Something Here

Date:_____

Things That Pissed Me Off Today

_____

_____

_____

_____

_____

_____

Things That Made Me Smile Today

_____

_____

_____

_____

_____

_____

My Mood Today

Scale of 1-8 (8 being, In A Very Bad Mood)

Today's Fucking Tasks

I'm So Glad I Didn't...

I'm So Relieved I Did..

SHIT I NEED TO DO TODAY

1
2
3
4
5

Date:_____

Things That Pissed Me Off Today

_____
_____
_____
_____
_____
_____

Things That Made Me Smile Today

_____
_____
_____
_____
_____
_____

My Mood Today

Scale of 1-8 (8 being, In A Very Bad Mood)

Today's Fucking Thoughts

People I Want To Strangle Today

Draw Something Here

Date:_____

Things That Pissed Me Off Today

_____

_____

_____

_____

_____

_____

Things That Made Me Smile Today

_____

_____

_____

_____

_____

_____

My Mood Today

Scale of 1-8 (8 being, In A Very Bad Mood)

Today's Fucking Tasks

I'm So Glad I Didn't...

I'm So Relieved I Did..

SHIT I NEED TO DO TODAY

1
2
3
4
5

Date:_____

Things That Pissed Me Off Today

_____

_____

_____

_____

_____

_____

Things That Made Me Smile Today

_____

_____

_____

_____

_____

_____

My Mood Today

👆 👆 👆 👆 👆 👆 👆 👆

Scale of 1-8 (8 being, In A Very Bad Mood)

Today's Fucking Thoughts

People I Want To Strangle Today

Draw Something Here

Date:_____

Things That Pissed Me Off Today

_____

_____

_____

_____

_____

_____

Things That Made Me Smile Today

_____

_____

_____

_____

_____

_____

My Mood Today

Scale of 1-8 (8 being, In A Very Bad Mood)

Today's Fucking Tasks

I'm So Glad I Didn't...

I'm So Relieved I Did..

SHIT I NEED TO DO TODAY

1
2
3
4
5

Date:_____

Things That Pissed Me Off Today

_____

_____

_____

_____

_____

_____

Things That Made Me Smile Today

_____

_____

_____

_____

_____

_____

My Mood Today

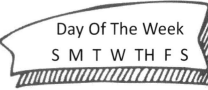

Scale of 1-8 (8 being, In A Very Bad Mood)

Today's Fucking Thoughts

People I Want To Strangle Today

Draw Something Here

Date:_____

Things That Pissed Me Off Today

_____

_____

_____

_____

_____

_____

Things That Made Me Smile Today

_____

_____

_____

_____

_____

_____

My Mood Today

Scale of 1-8 (8 being, In A Very Bad Mood)

Today's Fucking Tasks

I'm So Glad I Didn't...

I'm So Relieved I Did..

SHIT I NEED TO DO TODAY

1
2
3
4
5

Date:_____

Things That Pissed Me Off Today

_____
_____
_____
_____
_____
_____

Things That Made Me Smile Today

_____
_____
_____
_____
_____
_____

My Mood Today

Scale of 1-8 (8 being, In A Very Bad Mood)

Today's Fucking Thoughts

People I Want To Strangle Today

Draw Something Here

Date:_____

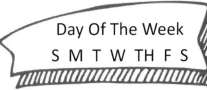
Things That Pissed Me Off Today

_____

_____

_____

_____

_____

_____

Things That Made Me Smile Today

_____

_____

_____

_____

_____

_____

My Mood Today

Scale of 1-8 (8 being, In A Very Bad Mood)

Today's Fucking Tasks

I'm So Glad I Didn't...

I'm So Relieved I Did..

SHIT I NEED TO DO TODAY

1
2
3
4
5

Date:_____

Things That Pissed Me Off Today

_____

_____

_____

_____

_____

_____

Things That Made Me Smile Today

_____

_____

_____

_____

_____

My Mood Today

Scale of 1-8 (8 being, In A Very Bad Mood)

Today's Fucking Thoughts

People I Want To Strangle Today

Draw Something Here

Date:_____

Things That Pissed Me Off Today

_____

_____

_____

_____

_____

_____

Things That Made Me Smile Today

_____

_____

_____

_____

_____

_____

My Mood Today

Scale of 1-8 (8 being, In A Very Bad Mood)

Today's Fucking Tasks

I'm So Glad I Didn't...

I'm So Relieved I Did..

SHIT I NEED TO DO TODAY

1
2
3
4
5

Date:_____

Things That Pissed Me Off Today

_____

_____

_____

_____

_____

_____

Things That Made Me Smile Today

_____

_____

_____

_____

_____

_____

My Mood Today

👆 👆 👆 👆 👆 👆 👆 👆

Scale of 1-8 (8 being, In A Very Bad Mood)

Today's Fucking Thoughts

People I Want To Strangle Today

Draw Something Here

Date:_____

Things That Pissed Me Off Today

_____

_____

_____

_____

_____

_____

Things That Made Me Smile Today

_____

_____

_____

_____

_____

_____

My Mood Today

Scale of 1-8 (8 being, In A Very Bad Mood)

Today's Fucking Thoughts

People I Want To Strangle Today

Draw Something Here

Manufactured by Amazon.ca
Bolton, ON